Native American Crafts
of the Plains and Plateau

By Judith Hoffman Corwin

Franklin Watts

A Division of Scholastic Inc.

New York Toronto London Auckland Sydney
Mexico City New Delhi Hong Kong
Danbury, Connecticut

For Jules Arthur and Oliver Jamie, and for the makers of these wondrous and beautiful things, who, through the ages, in many different ways, paint, sculpt, and sing of the Earth

I would also like to thank my editor, Lorna Greenberg, for all her generous help, support, and cheerful spirit.

Book design by A. Natacha Pimentel C.

Library of Congress Cataloging-in-Publication Data
Corwin, Judith Hoffman.
        Native American crafts of the Plains and Plateau / by Judith Hoffman Corwin.
              p. cm.
        Summary: Gives some historical background on Indian tribes of the Plains and Plateau and provides instructions for craft projects derived from their handicrafts, such as corncob dolls, headbands, and a handmade book.
        Includes index.
        ISBN 0-531-12202-6 (lib. bdg.)   0-531-15595-1 (pbk.)
        1. Indian craft—Juvenile literature. 2. Indians of North America—Industries—Great Plains—Juvenile literature. 3. Indians of North America—Industries—Northwest, Pacific—Juvenile literature. [1.Indian craft. 2. Handicraft.] I. Title.
TT22.C68 2002
745.5'08997—dc21   2001007265

Contents

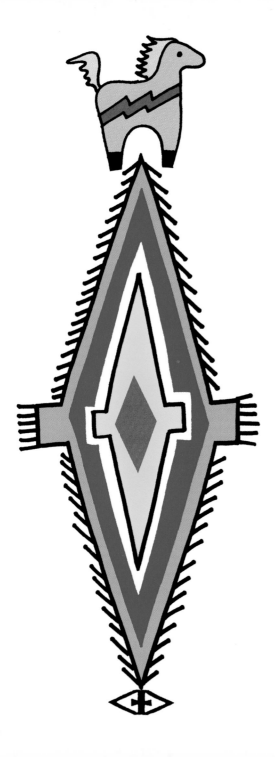

About the Native American Crafts Books

All things in this world
Have souls or spirits.
The sky has a spirit,
The clouds have spirits;
So have animals, trees, grass, water, stones,
Everything.

—Hidatsa

Native Americans are believed to have been the first people to arrive on the North American continent thousands of years ago. They developed rich cultures based on their respect for the natural world around them—the Earth, sky, wind, rain, animals, plants, fire and water, the sun, the moon, and the stars.

The spirit of nature is important to Native Americans, and the design and decoration of the objects they use in their daily lives—to raise families, to farm, to hunt, to defend themselves or to make war—reflect the elements of nature. The designs on their clothing, pottery, baskets, dwellings, and

5

weapons are decorative and are also an appeal to the goodwill of the spirits of the natural world. Native American people have no word for art because creating art is an integral part of life.

Now many Native Americans live in cities. Yet they often return to their home reservations to visit families and for special occasions. Their past is kept alive through storytelling and through arts and crafts. Traditional crafts, like the stories, are handed down from generation to generation, carrying along a cultural message.

The Native American Crafts series of books introduces young people to the cultures of Native Americans and to their creative work. We can learn about and appreciate Native American culture and incorporate what we learn into our lives through making art objects inspired by their examples. The projects in these books are based on crafts of everyday life, but do not involve ritual or religious objects.

Native Americans of the Plains and Plateau

The Plains

Long ago millions of buffalo roamed the grasslands of North America's Great Plains. Native American hunters followed the thundering herds. The Plains stretch from Texas to Canada, and from the Mississippi and Missouri Rivers to the Rocky Mountains. The region has fertile river valleys, prairies, lakes, seas of grasslands, and fields of wildflowers. Cottonwood and willow trees line the banks of the Missouri River. Elm, poplar, and box elder trees grow along the Red River's edge. Cranberries, wild rice, grapes, and plums once grew wild in the region. The buffalo, or bison, that wandered the area came to eat the sweet grasses.

The Native Americans who lived in the region all depended on the buffalo, their main source of food. They hunted the great herds of buffalo on horseback, wearing feather headdresses and colorful embroidered and beaded clothing. They also hunted deer, antelope, elk, bear, caribou, moose, wild sheep,

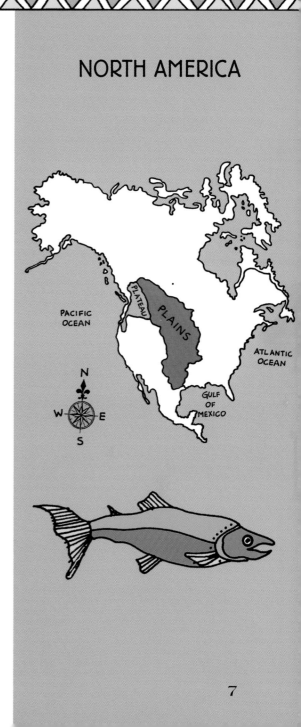

NORTH AMERICA

squirrels, rabbits, and possums, and gathered wild plants, seeds, and roots. The Plains tribes included the Cheyenne, Blackfoot, Arapaho, Crow, Dakota Sioux, Comanche, Gros Ventre, Omaha, Kiowa, Hidatsa, Pawnee, and Mandan. The Pawnee and Mandan also did some farming.

The Plateau

Native Americans of the Plateau lived in the upper Columbia River Basin on land that now forms the states of Washington, Oregon, Idaho, and Montana. They also lived in areas of British Columbia, between the Rocky Mountains on the east and the Cascade Mountains on the west. They fished for salmon in summer and fall, and gathered plants in the fertile valleys. In winter, they hunted deer, elk, moose, and bear. Some tribes traveled to the Plains each year to hunt buffalo. The Plateau tribes included the Nez Perce, Flathead, Kalispel, Wishram, Kotenai, and Thompson.

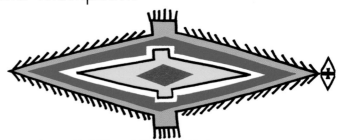

Today we learn about the importance of protecting our environment and the creatures that live in it. Our survival depends on them. The Plains and Plateau people, and other Native American groups, have always respected the land and its creatures.

Here's What You Need:
- paper, poster paints, brushes, colored pencils or markers, fabric markers
- T-shirt, cotton cloth, clay (page 47) or other materials

Plains and Plateau Designs and Symbols

Symbols are decorative marks or drawings that carry a special meaning. Native American designs and symbols have been passed down from one generation to another for centuries. They sometimes tell stories or include images from the spirit world or from dreams. Here are a variety of ancient and modern Native American designs. The symbols are based on traditional images that I have collected. You can use these and the decorative alphabet on page 41 for the projects in this book.

Experiment with the designs and draw them on T-shirts, stones, greeting cards, bookmarks, book covers, or stationery. Etch them on clay tablets or bowls. Fill a large cloth to make a mural or a wall hanging. Write a poem on a scroll or poster and decorate it. Write the title or the first letter of each line in the decorative alphabet. You can create your own design to use as your signature on art projects.

☀ Sun, life, warmth, glow	Smoke, change, truth
⌒ Sunrise, dawn, morning, hope, light	⊕ Four directions (North, East, South, West)
⌒ Sunset, end of day, evening	Arrow, movement, direction
★ Star, light, guidance	Double arrow, choice
☾ Moon, change	Crossed arrows, peace, guidance, help
☁ Cloud, air, sky, mist, fog	Inspiration, change, secret society
☁ Raincloud, rain, thunderstorm	⊙ Spiral, creation, earth, seasons
Rain, weather	△ Triangle, three, creation
Lightning, power, silver streak	♡ Heart, love
Sky	Feather, truth
Water, movement, change	Fish, water, stream, food
∞ Endless time, eternity, creativity, vision	Bird, travel, flight, freedom
▢ Square, equality	Horse, journey, speed
Crop cycle	

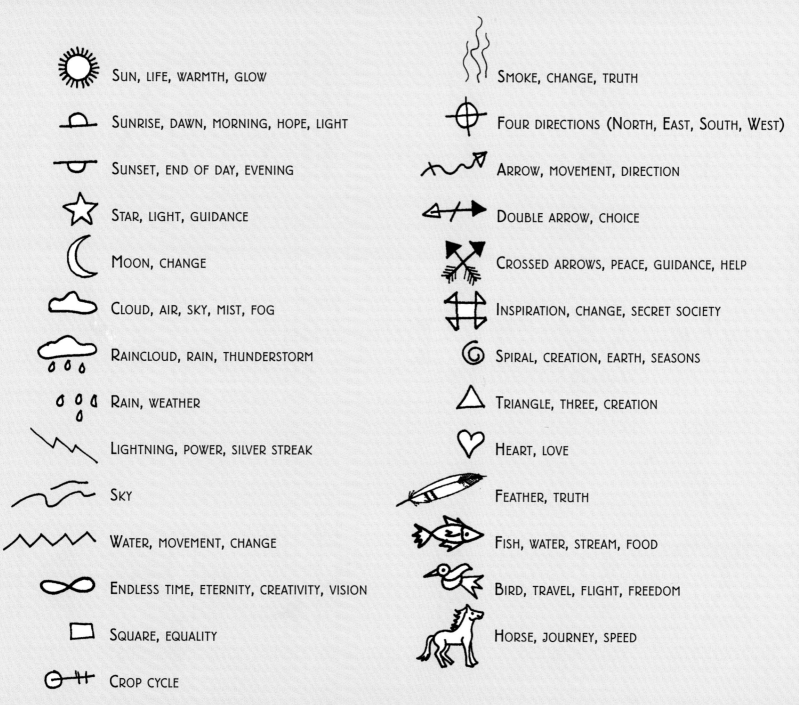

11

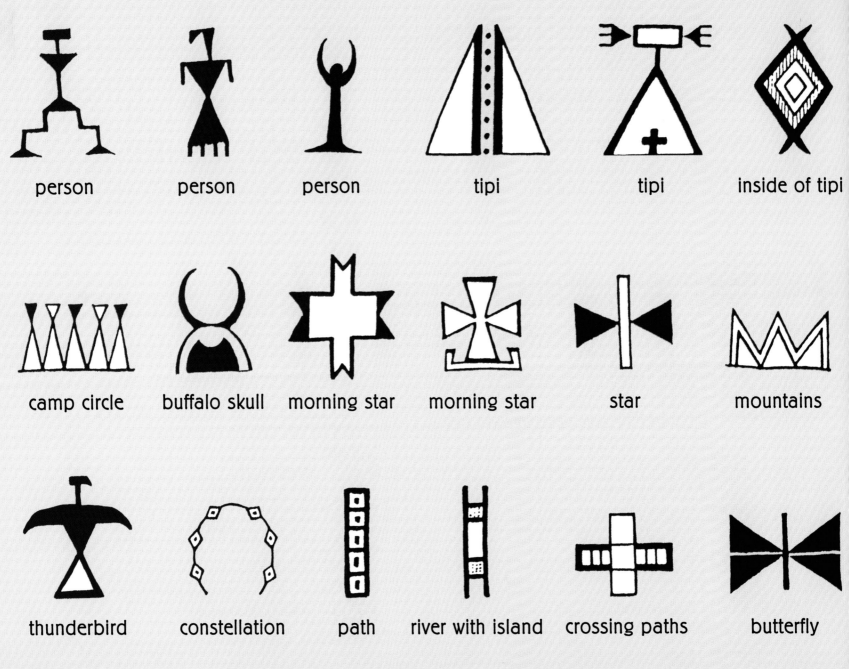

person	person	person	tipi	tipi	inside of tipi
camp circle	buffalo skull	morning star	morning star	star	mountains
thunderbird	constellation	path	river with island	crossing paths	butterfly

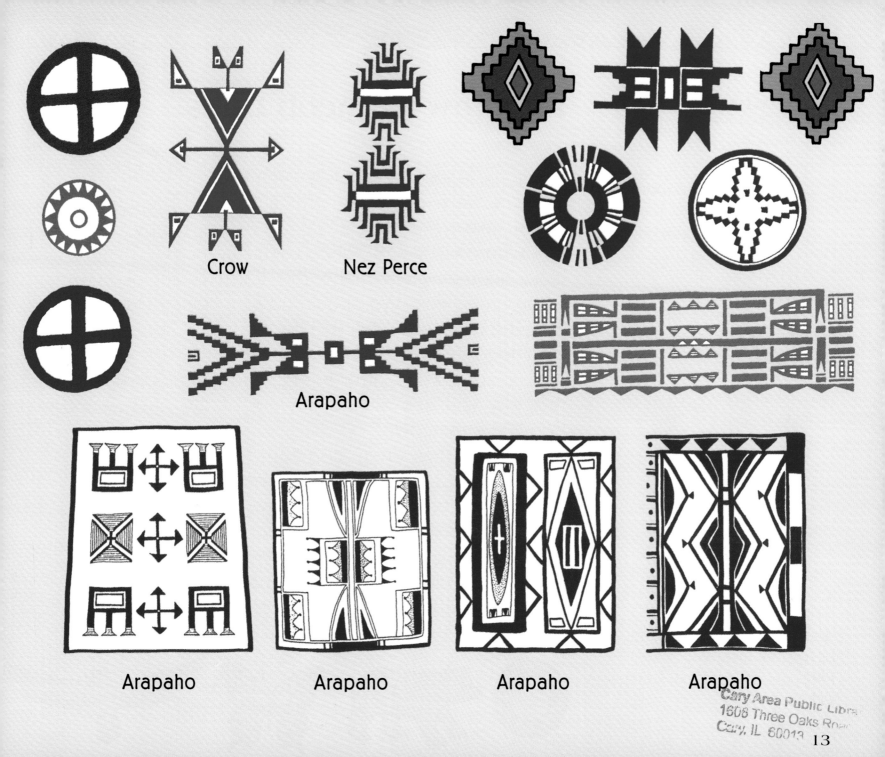

Crow

Nez Perce

Arapaho

Arapaho

Arapaho

Arapaho

Arapaho

13

Here's What You Need:

- one corncob for each doll
- colored markers
- brown or black yarn
- pencil, paper, scissors, glue, tape, plain paper towels
- white fabric, strips of colored fabric, string
- scraps of felt, suede, fake fur, leather, brown paper bag
- feathers, buttons, shells, beads, sequins, needle and thread

Here's How You Do It:

- Choose a design. With a black marker, draw eyes, a nose, and mouth on a corncob. Glue on yarn for hair. You can make a braid out of yarn and glue it on too.
- To make arms, take one sheet from a roll of paper towels and roll it tightly. Tape it closed and cut it in half. Glue the arms onto the corncob body. Trim them if they are too long. You can also make dolls without arms.

Rainbow Corncob Dolls

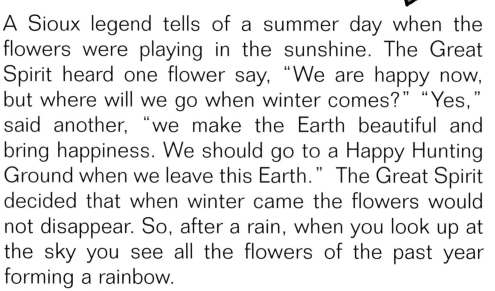

A Sioux legend tells of a summer day when the flowers were playing in the sunshine. The Great Spirit heard one flower say, "We are happy now, but where will we go when winter comes?" "Yes," said another, "we make the Earth beautiful and bring happiness. We should go to a Happy Hunting Ground when we leave this Earth." The Great Spirit decided that when winter came the flowers would not disappear. So, after a rain, when you look up at the sky you see all the flowers of the past year forming a rainbow.

We will use dried corncobs to make Native-American style dolls dressed in bright flower colors. There are designs for a rainbow princess, a chief, and a medicine person; and for dolls dressed in traditional Sioux, Crow, Blackfoot, Cheyenne, and Nez Perce clothing. (To get dried corncobs: save the cobs when you eat corn on the cob, and let them dry in the sun for a day or two.)

RAINBOW PRINCESS

CHIEF

MEDICINE PERSON

SIOUX

- To make a shirt, dress, robe, or pants, fold a piece of white fabric in half. With the fold at the top, draw the outline on the fabric. Cut it out. Cut out a neck or waist opening at the top. Add designs with markers, and glue on bits of suede, fake fur, sequins, or beads. Cut fringes at the bottom edges or glue on strips of felt or brown paper cut into fringes.
- Dress the corncob, using glue or ties where needed. Wrap a shawl around the princess and glue on button or shell decorations. String some beads for a necklace. The medicine person's robe could also be wrapped and glued on.
- You can draw small hands on felt. Cut them out and glue them inside the ends of the sleeves. You can add feet, too.

• For a headband, use a narrow strip of fabric. Glue or tape real or painted paper feathers or a cutout paper flower onto the fabric. Tie on the headband.

CROW

BLACKFOOT

CHEYENNE

NEZ PERCE

Natural World Memory Game

Young Native Americans needed skills to help them in the natural world. A keen eye was important for hunting. This game for two or more players will help you sharpen your skills. It uses game pieces with designs adapted from images familiar to Native Americans of the Plains and Plateau. Choose your designs from pages 11–12.

The object of the game is to collect the most pairs of matching game pieces. Here is how to play: Place all the game pieces facedown on the floor. Each player, in turn, turns over two pieces. If the pieces match, the player takes the pair and gets another turn. That player continues until he or she misses. If the pieces don't match, the player turns them facedown again in the same place. All the players try to remember the cards, to make a match in their turn.

When all the pieces have been matched, the game is over. The player with the most pairs wins. For an easier game, use 12 designs. For a harder game, use 30 (see page 12 for more designs).

Here's What You Need:
- oaktag
- ruler, pencil, scissors, black marker

Here's How You Do It:
- Cut out 40 strips of oaktag, each one 2 inches (5 cm) wide by 6 inches (15 cm) long.
- Choose 20 designs. With the black marker, draw the designs on the game pieces. Make two game pieces of each design. Leave the backs of the game pieces blank.

Here's What You Need:
- tape measure or a length of string, ruler, pencil, scissors
- strip of felt, chamois cloth (sold at hardware stores), or other heavy cloth 2 inches (5 cm) wide and about 25 inches (62 cm) long
- feathers or oaktag
- acrylic or poster paints and brushes, newspaper
- beads, string, glue

Here's How You Do It:
- Measure all around your head—just above your eyebrows—with a string or tape measure. Add 6 inches (15 cm) to that measurement. Cut a strip of fabric in the length you need.
- Choose designs from pages 11–13. Trace and transfer (page 46) them or draw them onto the headband. Center the designs on the headband, leaving 3 inches (8 cm) at each end blank. Color in the designs with paint.

Eagle Feathers and Headbands

The Plains and Plateau are home to many large birds, especially the eagle. This powerful creature is thought to have links to the heavenly spirits. Its feathers are often used on ceremonial costumes and headdresses. We will make eagle-feather headbands.

18

- If you have real feathers, paint the edges with acrylic or poster paint. (Acrylic paint can stain, so cover your work area with newspaper.) Or cut out feathers from oaktag and paint them. Tie a string or strip of cloth to the feathers and paint it. Add some beads to the string if you like.
- Tape or glue the feathers to the inside of the headband, or slip them into the knot after you tie on the headband. If you like, knot some beads onto the ends of a few strings. Glue the other ends of the strings to the headband. Tie the headband around your head.

19

Here's What You Need:
- homemade clay (page 47)
- pencil, scissors
- poster or acrylic paints and brushes, newspaper
- fake fur, yarn, thread, chamois cloth, string,
- white glue, cardboard

Here's How You Do It:
- Take a large handful of clay and shape a miniature buffalo. Start by making a rough shape of the head, large chest, and body and legs. After you finish the shape, stand it up on a table and press down lightly so that the body is supported by the legs.
- Shape the animal's ears. With a pencil, carve eyes and a mouth.
- Bake the buffalo (page 47). When cool, paint it brown. If you use acrylic paint, protect your work surfaces with newspaper.

Wild Woolly Buffalo

The huge buffalo that roamed the Great Plains many years ago were a symbol of this wild country. Native Americans who lived in this area depended on the animal. It was their main source of food. They used its hide for clothing, to make tipis, to make shields and drums, and for carryalls. We will make a furry clay buffalo.

- Glue on bits of tan and brown fake fur, yarn, thread, or chamois cloth for a shaggy coat. Glue on a string tail.
- Paint a piece of cardboard to look like prairie grass and glue the buffalo onto it.

Here's What You Need:
- chamois cloth, cotton cloth, an old sheet, or brown Kraft paper
- tape, pencil, fine-line black marker, scissors
- colored markers or paints and brushes

Here's How You Do It:
- Draw the outline of the buffalo hide shape on your cloth. Tape the cloth to a flat surface such as a tabletop.
- Choose drawings from pages 23–25 to make up your buffalo hunt scene. Trace and transfer (see page 46) the designs to the cloth, or draw them freehand.
- Go over the designs with a black marker and then color them in.
- Remove the tape and cut out the buffalo hide shape.

Buffalo Hide Painting

In earlier times, Native Americans of the Plains recorded important events—such as a successful hunt or a battle—in paintings on buffalo hide. First, the animal skin was tanned and treated with a glue-like paint to preserve the color and protect it from dirt. Outlines of the figures were scratched on with a sharpened stone, bone, or stick. Then they were painted in with paints made from minerals and plants, and a buffalo-tail paintbrush. We will make a buffalo hunt scene with plenty of action and detail. You can paint it on a piece of cloth shaped like a buffalo hide, or on a shirt. Or you might enlarge the drawing (using a copying machine) to make a wall hanging.

25

Here's What You Need:

- homemade clay (page 47) and extra flour for the work surface
- tracing paper, pencil, scissors, butter knife
- large needle or paper clip
- poster or acrylic paints and brushes, newspaper
- clay or store-bought beads, string
- feathers or paper or felt, glue, silver marker

Here's How You Do It:

- Sprinkle some flour on a clean working surface. Place the clay on the surface and flatten it until it is about 1 inch (2.5 cm) thick.
- Trace the outline of the horse (page 46). Cut it out and place the pattern on the clay. Draw around it with a pencil. With a knife, cut out the clay horse.

Moondrop Crazy Horse

In the sixteenth century, Spanish explorers brought horses with them from Europe. In the Southwest, Native Americans fought the Spanish who wanted their land. Many people died and many horses ran off into the wild. In time, herds of wild horses spread northward into the Plains. The Plains people began to capture and tame the wild horses.

On horseback, the Sioux could hunt down many buffalo and could travel to distant hunting grounds. The Plains people transported their belongings on a travois—a kind of sled pulled by dogs. Horses could pull heavier loads. The horses also carried saddlebags, in which belongings were stored. A fast horse was a prized possession and a companion. The horses were honored for helping in the hunt and delivering their riders safely home. The horses, like the best hunters, were treated well and decorated with eagle feathers. We will make a clay horse, and name it Moondrop Crazy Horse.

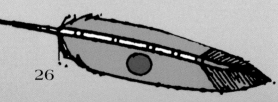

26

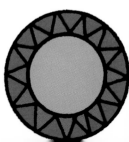

- Bake the horse (page 47). When it is cool, paint it a solid color. If you use acrylic paint, spread newspaper over the work surface.
- Tie a string to the horse's mane and attach a few beads at the ends. To make beads from clay, roll out some pea-sized balls. With an opened paper clip or a needle, make a hole in each bead large enough for your string to go through. Bake the beads, let them cool, and paint them.
- Glue on some small feathers to decorate the horse's mane. You can draw feathers on paper, cut them out, and paint them.
- Paint on the details. With a silver marker add the pattern on the horse's coat.

The Story of the Ghost Hunter

—Adapted from a Dakota Sioux Folktale

The Dakota, the largest group of Sioux people, lived west of the Great Lakes. The Dakota custom was to always hunt in groups—never alone. After a successful hunt, everything was shared with all the members of the tribe.

One winter a hunter went out to hunt alone. His family was starving and he did not want to share with the others after the hunt. He set off into the forest, made camp, and built a fire. He curled up to sleep, but was disturbed by a loud howl echoing through the forest. Then a ghost with glowing eyes appeared. The terrified hunter closed his eyes, but could sense the ghost circling around him. Forcing his eyes open, he saw not a ghost, but a large and fierce wolf.

The moon shone down on the hunter and the menacing wolf. In a flash, the hunter understood that the ghost-wolf had appeared because he had ignored the Dakota custom. The wolf led the hunter to a nearby camp where hunters from another tribe were gathered around a fire. The wolf stared at the lone hunter, then at the group of hunters, and walked into the fire. He came out the other side unharmed—and turned into a man. The ghost-man asked the hunters to allow the lone hunter to join them. He then changed back into a wolf, slid into the dark forest, and disappeared into the night.

The lone hunter joined the group and never hunted alone again. He became a skilled hunter, bringing plenty of food to his family and his tribe. Whenever he hunted, he left some meat at the edge of the forest. In the morning light, the meat was gone— only a wolf's footprints remained.

We will use this story in the next project. Or you could write it out and put it into a handmade book (see page 34). ◈

Here's What You Need:
- old solid-color sweatshirt
- chamois cloth, tan Ultrasuede, or felt
- pencil, scissors, glue
- black permanent marker, colored markers
- beads, needle, strong thread (buttonhole or quilting) or dental floss

Here's How You Do It:
- Cut off the the sweatshirt's cuffs, waistband, and neckband.
- Trace and transfer (page 46) the wolf design onto the shirt. With a black permanent marker draw over the pencil lines. Color in the design.
- Now we will add fringes around the neck and the cuffs, along the bottom, and down the front on each side of the wolf design.

Ghost Hunter Fringed Shirt

Native Americans are natural artists who draw inspiration and ideas from their surroundings. A beautiful sunset is reflected in the colors of a necklace, or the decoration of a tipi. The outline of a bird in flight becomes a dramatic symbol. The objects they make are cultural messengers, preserving traditional images and customs. A craftsperson works from the heart, to the head, to the hand.

We will make a Ghost Hunter shirt from an old sweatshirt. The wolf of the Ghost Hunter story will be the central design.

- Cut lengths of chamois cloth, Ultrasuede, or felt, 3 inches (8 cm) wide and 15 inches (38 cm) long. If the strips are shorter, you can add pieces. Glue the strips to the shirt.
- When the glue is dry, make cuts all along the strips, about 1/4 inch (6 mm) apart.
- If you like, sew on a bead design. Cut a 20 inch (50 cm) length of strong thread or dental floss. Pull the thread through a needle and knot the ends. Push the needle up from the inside of the shirt. Put four beads on the needle. Push the needle down into the shirt (near the neck) and then up again. Put four more beads on the needle and repeat. Continue until you have made a pattern around the neck. Push the needle down into the shirt. Make a knot and cut off the needle.

Here's What You Need:

- 22 by 18 inch (55 by 45 cm) sheet of white oaktag or a brown paper bag cut to size
- scissors, pencil
- fine-line black marker, colored markers or poster paints and brushes
- glue, strings, beads

Here's How You Do It:

- Draw the envelope shape on the oaktag or paper bag. Cut it out.
- Trace and transfer (page 46) the designs onto the envelope. Go over the pencil lines with a fine-line black marker. Color in the designs with colored markers or paint.
- Fold up the bottom edge of the envelope, leaving the flap at the top.
- Glue the sides together.
- If you like, add some strings with beads attached. Fold down the flap.

Comanche Parfleche

A parfleche is a folder or carrying case used by Plains Indians. It is made from a piece of rawhide that is cut and folded into a large envelope. The edges are sewn together with strips of rawhide. The folder is decorated with tribal designs. Two folders can be attached to the ends of a rawhide strip to make saddlebags. Parfleche comes from the French phrase *parer une flèche*, meaning, "to turn aside an arrow." You can make a handsome parfleche to hold special papers or photographs.

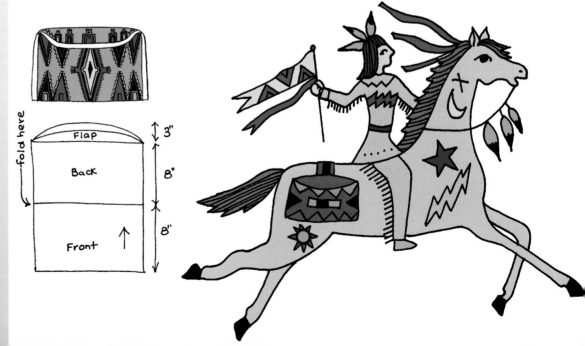

flap design

parfleche design

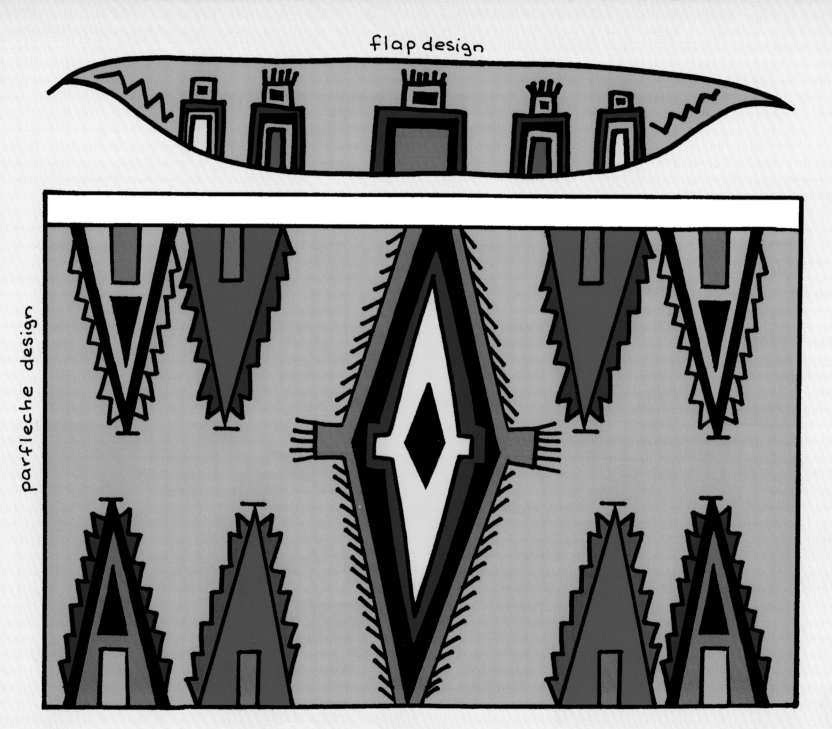

Here's What You Need:
- ruler, pencil, scissors, tracing paper
- large brown paper bag (if it has printing on it, turn it inside out)
- five sheets of typing paper
- hole punch, 6 inch (15 cm) twig
- two 6 inch (15 cm) pieces of string, yarn, or rope
- colored pencils or markers

Here's How You Do It:
- With a ruler, outline a 9 by 12 inch (22.5 by 30 cm) rectangle on the paper bag. Cut it out.
- Fold the sheets of white paper in half the long way. Fold the paper bag in half the long way and slip it over the folded sheets to make a book.
- Punch out two holes—one 2 inches (5 cm) from the top of the book and another 2 inches (5 cm) from the bottom.

Coyote Sings to the Moon Handmade Book

A coyote is a Native American prairie wolf, a member of the canine—or dog—family. Coyotes have coarse brownish-yellow fur and long straight tails. In folklore, the coyote often appears as a trickster. In a Lakota Sioux legend, the coyote taught the people how to sing. The coyote was a common sight on the prairie, howling at the moon. We will make a handmade book with a singing coyote on the cover. You can write Native American verses inside (pages 44–45) and decorate the pages.

- Place a twig on top of the book along the folded edge. Insert a string into the top hole, through the book, and out the back. Tie the ends of the string to hold the twig, book cover, and pages together. Put the second string through the bottom hole and tie it. Leave the ends of the strings free.
- Trace and transfer (page 46) the coyote design to the front of the book cover. Color it in. Add other designs.

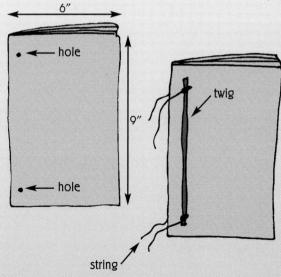

Here's What You Need:
- pencil, scissors, 7 1/2 inch (19 cm) paper plate
- 8 1/2 by 11 inch (21 by 28 cm) white paper
- homemade clay (page 47)
- straws or twigs, 12 inches (30 cm) long
- tape, rubber bands, white glue, toothpick
- colored pencils or markers
- 8 inch (20 cm) square of oaktag or cardboard
- large oaktag sheet

Here's How You Do It:
- Place the plate facedown on a sheet of paper and draw around it. Cut out the circle you have drawn. Fold it in half, then cut along the fold.
- Take one half-circle and pull the corners together to make a cone. Tape the edges together. This is your tipi. The other half-circle can be used for a second tipi.
- Place a tipi on the cardboard and draw around it.

Tipis of the Plains

Let all believe as they wish.
Never destroy the land and its beauty.
No one is responsible for another's bad deeds.
Thank the Great Spirit for each day.
Never give your word unless you can keep it.
In others' lodges, follow their ways.

These traditional customs and others are respected in Native American homes. The home for most Plains people was a cone-shaped tent called a tipi. The tipi was lightweight, waterproof, and could be carried along to a new campsite when the people moved to follow the buffalo herds. We will make a miniature tipi like those of the Plains people.

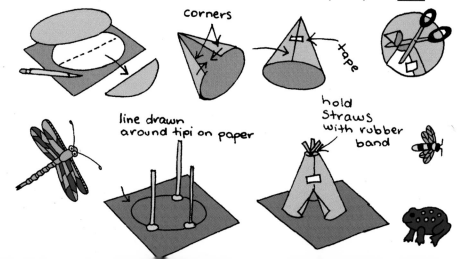

corners

tape

hold straws with rubber band

line drawn around tipi on paper

Actual size tipi with decorations

- Pinch off three pea-sized pieces of clay. Place them around the circle drawn on the cardboard.
- Push a straw or twig into each clay ball. Pull the tops of the three straws together and secure them with a rubber band. Slip the paper cone over the straws. Make a doorway, as shown, and fold the edges back.
- Choose designs and draw them or trace and transfer them (page 46) onto a sheet of paper. Color them in. Cut them out and glue them onto the tipi. Draw on border decorations. Look at this page and page 38 for ideas.
- Put a little glue on a toothpick and run it along the bottom of the tipi. Press the tipi onto the cardboard base.
- It might be fun to make a whole encampment. Draw a large circle on a sheet of oak-tag to form a base for your tipi camp.

37

38

Sign Language Communicating

As the Native American tribes moved across the Plains, the people broke into smaller groups and the way they spoke gradually changed. Many languages developed. In time, when tribes met, they did not speak the same language. So they created a way of talking with their hands—a sign language—that all Plains people could understand.

Native American sign language is like picture writing. The gestures carry meaning. Signs show if people are friendly or hostile. Chiefs made peace agreements with signs. People shared information— where to find water, where tribes camped, and other matters. Mandan farmers used signs when trading corn for Sioux buffalo skins.

Try out the sign language gestures on page 40 with your friends. Use one or both hands.

SIGN LANGUAGE COMMUNICATING

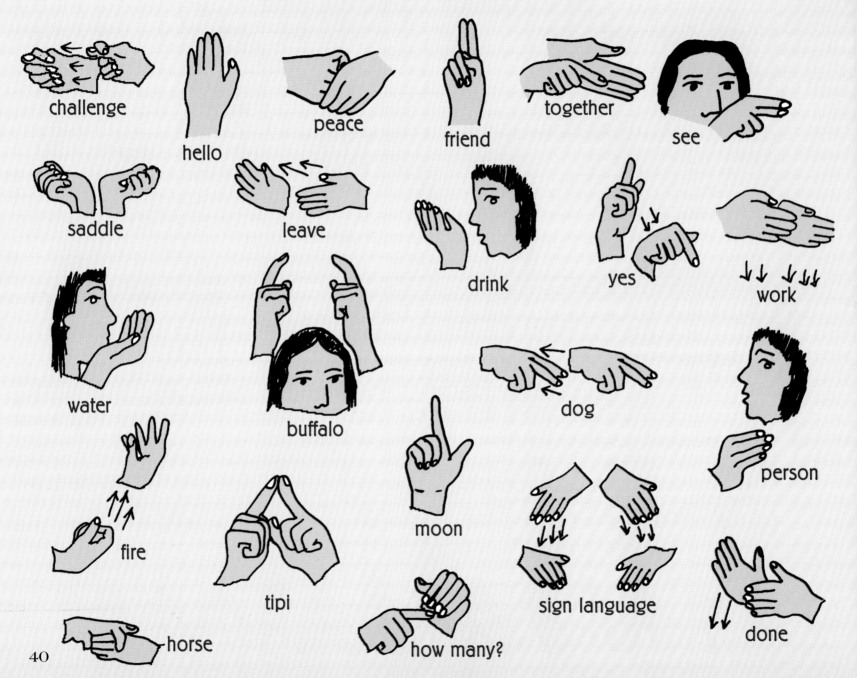

challenge

hello

peace

friend

together

see

saddle

leave

drink

yes

work

water

buffalo

drink

dog

person

fire

tipi

moon

sign language

done

horse

how many?

Native American Decorative Alphabet

This decorative alphabet is based on ancient Native American symbols. Use the letters to write a story or poem title, or as a secret code. You can use them to write your name or initials on a shirt or cap, or a scrapbook cover, or in a handmade book (page 34).

(page 34)

Here's What You Need:
- black or red fine-line marker, permanent fabric markers
- paper, fabric, or other materials

Here's How You Do It:
- Practice drawing the letters on paper with a fine-line marker.
- Draw the letters on paper, fabric, or whatever material you choose. Use permanent fabric markers on cloth.

A B C D E F G H I
J K L M N O P Q
R S T U V W X Y Z

41

Here's What You Need:
- 1 cup sifted flour
- 1 cup yellow cornmeal
- 3 tablespoons sugar
- 4 teaspoons baking powder
- 1 1/2 teaspoons salt
- 1 egg, beaten
- 1 1/2 cups milk
- 1 cup of canned corn, drained
- 1/4 cup butter, melted, plus extra butter to grease the pan
- 1/4 cup of your favorite berries
- measuring cups and spoons
- large mixing bowl and spoon
- 8 by 8 by 2 inch (20 by 20 by 5 cm) pan
- potholders, knife

Here's How You Do It:
- Ask an adult to help you use the oven. Preheat the oven to 350° F. (175° C.). Grease the pan and put it aside.

Berry and Corn Bread

Many of the early Plains people were farmers. The Mandan and the Pawnee lived in villages and grew corn and other crops in summer. In the fall they hunted buffalo, deer, and antelope. Corn is an important part of the Native American diet. It is eaten plain, and used in many recipes. It is pounded into powdery flour and used in corn bread.

- In the mixing bowl, combine the ingredients. Mix them thoroughly. Pour the batter into the pan and bake for 25 minutes, or until the top of the bread is golden brown.
- Remove from the oven. Cut into 16 squares and serve while it is still warm.

43

Here's What You Need:
- heavyweight paper
- black fine-line marker, colored markers or pencils

Here's How You Do It:
- Select a poem and write it on paper with the fine-line marker.
- Make a border using designs from this book. Experiment. Use different colored pencils or markers.

Native American Writings

These story-poems, songs, and chants have been adapted from traditional Native American pieces from various tribes. They give us a glimpse of another world in another time. You can write them on paper and add designs, or write them in a handmade book (page 34).

Story of the Seventh Direction
Wakan Tanka, the Great Spirit, created the Six Directions—East, South, West, North, Above, and Below.
Then he needed to create the Seventh Direction— the greatest of all, containing wisdom and strength. Wakan Tanka, the Great Spirit, wanted to put it somewhere it could not easily be found. He placed it in each person's heart.

—Lakota

My horse be swift
Even like a bird.
My horse be swift in flight,
Bear me now in safety
Far from the enemy's arrows,
And you shall be rewarded
With streamers and red ribbons.

—Sioux warrior's song to his horse

Brother Skunk
My tail rattles,
My ears rattle,
Each end rattles.
My whole body rattles.
My face is striped.
My back is striped.

—Mandan

I Sing for the Animals
Out of the Earth
I sing for them.
A horse nation
I sing for them.
Out of the Earth
I sing for them.
The animals
I sing for them.

—Sioux

45

Basic Techniques

Tracing Designs

Here's What You Need:
- tracing paper
- pencil, tape
- drawing paper, fabric, or other material

Here's How You Do It:
- Place tracing paper over the design you want to trace. If you like, tape the paper down. Trace the lines of the design, pressing firmly on your pencil.
- Remove the tape and turn the paper over. On the back, draw over the lines of the design with the side of your pencil point.
- Turn the tracing paper right side up and place it on a sheet of drawing paper or the material for your project. You may tape this down. Draw over the lines. This will transfer the design onto the paper or the material.

Making Clay

Here's What You Need:
- 2 cups flour plus extra flour to sprinkle on the work surface
- 1 cup salt
- 1 cup water
- large bowl, spoon, measuring cup
- cookie sheet, potholders, aluminum foil

Here's How You Do It:
- Use this recipe to make clay for projects in this book. Additional instructions are given with the specific projects.
- Mix the flour and salt in a bowl. Add the water a little at a time. Mix the clay well with your hands until it is smooth. The clay is ready to roll out and cut, or to shape according to the project directions.
- If you need to bake the clay, ask an adult to help you use the oven. Heat the oven to 325° F. (165° C.). Line a cookie sheet with aluminum foil and place the clay pieces on it, spacing them 1 inch (2.5 cm) apart. Bake until lightly browned, 15 to 20 minutes, but check often to see that the edges are not burning.
- Using potholders, remove the cookie sheet from the oven. Allow the clay to cool. Paint or decorate it following the project instructions.

Index